MW00893811

XML Programming Success in a Day

By Sam Key

Beginner's Guide to Fast, Easy, and Efficient Learning of XML Programming

2nd Edition

Copyright 2015 by Sam Key - All rights reserved.

Table Of Contents

Introduction

I want to thank you and congratulate you for purchasing the book, *"XML Programming Success in a Day"* .

This book contains proven steps and strategies on how to do XML programming.

Even if you are not knowledgeable about computers and programming, this book will help you understand what XML is all about. It will also help you discover its potential. Remember, XML is among the most powerful markup languages that you can learn without being a true-blue technology expert.

Thanks again for purchasing this book, I hope you enjoy it!

Chapter 1 What is XML Programming?

XML, or Extensible Markup Language, is recognized as a technical revolution that is almost comparable to the invention of the wheel and sliced bread. It is probably the most hyped technology in the late 1990's up to the present, though Java is a close second.

So what is the big deal about XML? For one, you can use it to make your Web applications more powerful, more versatile, and smarter.

What is XML?

You know now that XML stands for Extensible Markup Language. XML is text-based and derived from the Standard Generalized Markup Language or SGML.

XML tags identify, organize, and store data. It is not the same as the HTML tags which display the data. There is no way that XML would replace HTML in the future, however, it introduces a lot of possibilities by adopting some useful features of HTML.

So basically, XML is both a hardware-independent and software-independent tool used to carry information. Even though it is a markup language that is very similar to HTML, it is an entirely different entity. XML was designed to focus on the data while HTML was designed to focus on the appearance of the data. XML describes the data while HTML displays the data. XML is all about carrying information while HTML is about displaying the information.

In addition, XML is designed to be self-descriptive. In order to be highly efficient in XML, it is important for you to have at least a basic understanding of HTML and JavaScript. The tags in XML are also not predefined. Hence, you need to define your own tags.

5

Take a look at the following example:

```
<note>
    <to> Jane </to>
    <from> John </from>
    <heading> Memo </heading>
    <body> Come to the meeting at ten o'clock in the morning
    tomorrow. </body>
</note>
```

As you can see, the example given above is quite self-descriptive. You can see the information about both the sender and the receiver. It also contains a heading and a message body. Nevertheless, you should realize that this XML document is merely information that contains tags. It does not have a specific function. In other words, it is useless and does not do anything important. In order for you to be able to send, display, or receive this note, you need to use a software program.

In XML, you define your own tags. Using the example given above, you can see that the tags are not defined in a particular XML standard. The tags are "invented" by the author of the document. As a programmer, you have the freedom to invent whatever tags you like. You also have the freedom to create your own document structure.

XML is a language that does not have any predefined tags. HTML, on the other hand, has predefined tags that you need to use in your codes. Documents in HTML are only allowed to use the tags defined in the HTML standard, such as <h1> and <p>.

There are three characteristics of XML, as can be deduced from its name:

Extensible

XML allows you to characterize your own tags to make them suitable to your applications. It also enables you to extend the concept of what a document is: a file that lives on a file server. It can also be a temporary piece of data flowing between different Web services.

Markup

The tags or elements are the most familiar feature of XML. The XML elements that you will be creating will be comparable to the elements that you have been used to using in HTML documents. The only difference is that with XML, you are able to define your own set of tags or elements.

Language

The language used in XML and HTML are almost identical, but XML is more flexible as it gives you the chance to make your own tags. XML is more than just a language. It is a meta-language, meaning it allows you to create and define other languages. For instance, you can use XML to create languages like RSS and MAthML (Mathematical Markup Language).

Do You Need XML?

You need XML because HTML is used specifically to illustrate documents for display in the Web browser, nothing else. HTML becomes bulky when you try to display documents using your mobile device or anything that is quite complicated, like translating German content to English. The only purpose of HTML is to enable you to speedily create Web documents that you can effortlessly share with other people.

XML can be used in different contexts aside from the Web, such as in Web Services and other applications.

HTML rarely gives you information on how your document is prepared or gives you its meaning.

For the non-computer expert, HTML is simply a presentation language, while XML is a data-description language.

Here's the usual kind of code you will see by inspecting the structure of an e-commerce site's product listing:

```
<!DOCTYPE html PUBLIC "-//Business//DTD XHTML 1.0
Transitional//EN"
                "http://www.business.com/TR/xhtml1/DTD/xhtml1-
transitional.dtd">
<html xmlns="http://www.business.com/1999/xhtml">
<head>
<title>Shop Items</title>
<meta http-equiv="Content-Type"
  content="text/html; charset=iso-8859-1" />
</head>
<body>
<h1>Shop Items</h1>
<h2>Item A</h2>
<p>Item A is a remarkable tool that can make your chores much
easier.</p>
<p><b>Price: $35.00</b></p>
<p><b>Shipping: $8.00</b></p>
<h2>Item B</h2>
...
<h3>Item C</h3>
<p><i>Price: $55.99</i></p>
```

```
<p>This is so wonderful that you will never regret buying it .</p>

...

</body>

</html>
```

Learning About the Semantics and Jargons

Semantics is the study of the meaning of any language. It's a fact that humans are better at semantics compared to computers, simply because humans are excellent in deriving meanings. There is always a meaning in every action or language; for humans, it is easy to draw conclusions on what they are presented in front of them.

For instance, you were asked to list down as many names for female animals as you can, you are most likely begin with *doe, tigress, lioness,* or *ewe.* On the other hand, if you were given a list of names with categories, you are more than likely going to say *female animals.* In addition, if you were asked what a lioness is, you'll immediately say "a female lion."

From the above illustrations, computers do not have the capability to do that. It's a shame, though, since a lot of computing tasks need semantic skill. In this regard, computers need help.

Using the above example, it is highly likely that you can figure out that the <h> tag is used to tag a product name in their list. Also, you might be able to interpret that the 1st paragraph after <h2> is the product description, and the following 2 paragraphs indicate the price and shipping fee.

However, if you further look into it, even the cursory glance reveals significant human errors. Still using the above document, the last product name is visible in <h3> but not in <h2> tags.

A computer program or software that attempted to decode the document, but cannot make the kinds of semantic leaps needed to decipher the above statement, will ultimately fail. The computer will only be able to render the document to a browser with the styles that are associated with the tags. HTML is basically a set of instructions for rendering any kind of document in the Web browser, but it doesn't have the capability to structure and decode the meaning of each tag.

If the document above is created using XML, this might be what you will get:

```
<?xml version="1.0"?>
<productListing title="Shop Items">
 <product>
  <name>Item A</name>
  <description>Item A is an incredible brush that can
   make your hair shiner.</description>
  <cost>$88.40</cost>
  <shipping>$7.00</shipping>
 </product>
```

```
<product>
  <name>Item B</name>
  ...
</product>
<product>
  <name>Item C</name>
  <description>This is something so terrific that you will want
    it in your home or office! </p>
  <cost>$89.50</cost>
  <shipping>$7.00</shipping>
</product>
  ...
</productListing>
```

There really isn't anything new in the new document and obviously, there is no information about the display.

Also, have you ever wondered how a <product> tag would appear in a browser? Remember that when you use XML, you will be able to separate the information from the actual presentation.

Using XML

XML can be used in various aspects of Web development. It is typically used for storing and sharing data.

11

XML separates data from HTML. In case you have to show dynamic data in an HTML document, you have to edit it every time your data changes. Obviously, this takes a lot of time and effort.

With XML, however, you can store your data in separate files. This is much more convenient since you can focus on using CSS/HTML for your layout and display. You can also guarantee that the changes you make in your underlying data do not require changes to the HTML. Moreover, with a few codes in JavaScript, you can read external XML files as well as update the content of your Web page.

In the virtual world, computer databases and systems may see to contain data in compatible formats. This is not the case in the real world, though. XML data are actually stored in plain text format in order to provide a hardware-independent and software-independent way for storing data as well as make it easier to produce data that are sharable by various applications.

Just like many other Web developers, you may also have a hard time exchanging data between systems that are not compatible. Doing so can take a lot of your time and energy. Fortunately, with XML, you can simplify data transport. You can avoid experiencing too much complexity if you exchange data as XML because the data is readable even by incompatible and different applications.

Likewise, XML simplifies platform changes. As you know, upgrading to a new system, whether it is software or hardware platform, is time consuming. What's more, incompatible data is frequently lost when huge amounts of data have to be converted. Because of this, a lot of developers get frustrated. They waste time and energy, and they do not get the output that they hoped for.

With XML, you can store data in text format so you can quickly upgrade or expand to a new operating system, browser, or application without worrying that you might lose data.

XML also makes data more available. With XML, any kind of reading machine can access your data. Voice machines, handheld computers, and news feeds can all access your data from data sources in XML and in HTML pages. Even people with certain disabilities can easily access your data. Blind individuals, for instance, will not have a hard time accessing your content.

Many Internet languages are actually written in XML. Some of these include XML Schema, XHTML, SVG, RSS, and WSDL.

Chapter 2 Basic Syntax

This section will give you information on simple syntax rules when writing an XML document.

The following is a complete student uniform.

```
<?xml version="1.0"?>

<contact-info>

<name>Manny Dunphy</name>

<company>Real Realtor</company>

<phone>(895) 444-111</phone>

</contact-info>
```

You will see 2 kinds of information in this example:

- Markup - *<contact-info>*
- Text (character data) – Manny Dunphy and *(895) 444-111*

This diagram will give you the syntax rules in writing different types of markup and text with XML.

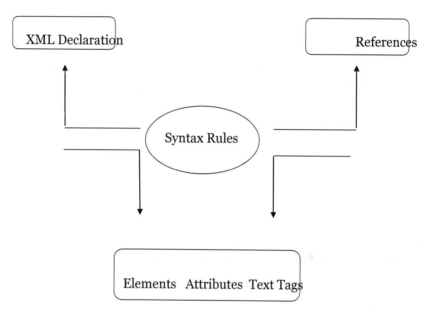

XML Declaration

The document may or may not have XML declaration. It can be written like this:

```
<?xml version="1.0" encoding="UTF-8"?>
```

Version is the XML version and other specific encoding specifies that the character encoding used in this particular document.

There's no need to worry if that's a bit unclear. You will learn more about XML declaration later.

Elements and Tags

XML elements are known as the building blocks of an XML. They behave as containers holding any of the following: the text, the elements, the attributes, the media objects - basically everything. Each document may contain one or more elements, the scopes can be delimited by start and end tags, or empty elements (with empty-element tag).

Syntax

<element-name attribute1 attribute2>

....content

</element-name>

Element name refers to the name of the element, and the case in the beginning and end tags should match.

Attribute 1, attribute 2 are the element attributes that are separated by the white spaces. Attribute refers to the property of the element. It is associated with a name and value, written like this:

name = "value"

Empty Element

An element without content appears like this:

An XML document with different XML elements will have this syntax:

<?xml version="1.0"?>

<contact-info>

    <address category="business">
        <name>Manny Dunphy</name>

        <company>Real Realtor</company>

        <phone>(895) 444-111</phone>

<address/>

</contact-info>

Rules

- The *name* should have alphanumeric characters with only these punctuation marks: the hyphen (-), underscore (_), and a period (.).

- They are case sensitive: *Address* and *address* are not the same.

- The beginning and end tags should match.

- The element may contain text or elements.

Comments in XML

In XML, the syntax for writing comments is the same as that of HTML. This is the syntax for a comment in XML:

<!—An example of a comment -->

Comments generally start with <!—and end with -->. They can contain any data with the exception of the string literal --. You are allowed to put comments between markups anywhere in your XML document.

New Line in XML

Applications in Windows generally store new lines as carriage return and line feed (CR + LF). Old Mac systems store a new line as carriage return while Mac OSX and Unix store it as line feed. XML, on the other hand, stores it as line feed.

Whitespace in XML

Unlike in HTML, multiple whitespaces in documents are not truncated in XML. HTML actually truncates multiple whitespaces into a single whitespace.

Chapter 3 XML Attributes, References, and Texts

Attributes are part of the elements. Every element may contain multiple and unique attributes. The attribute specifies a single property for the element, with the use of a name and value or name pair. The XML-elements can have one or more attributes:

Syntax

<element-name attribute1 attribute2 >

....content..

< /element-name>

Wherein *attribute1* and *attribute2* appear like this:

name = "value"

Value may be inside a (' ') or a double (" ") quote. Attributes are needed to add a distinctive label to an element, put the label in a category, add a Boolean flag, or associate with a string of data.

Use of Attributes

<?xml version="1.0" encoding="UTF-8"?>

```
<!DOCTYPE farm [

    <!ELEMENT farm (vegetables)*>

    <!ELEMENT vegetables (#PCDATA)>

    <!ATTLIST vegetables category CDATA #REQUIRED>
]>

<farm>

    <vegetables category="pumpkin" />   -empty elements

    <vegetables category="tomato">

    </vegetables>

</farm>
```

Attributes distinguish the elements with the same names. An attribute may add a tiny detail to differentiate two or more elements with the same name.

In this example, the vegetables were categorized with the inclusion of the *attribute category* and the use of varying values to each of the elements, giving you two *vegetable categories* one *pumpkin*, and one *tomato.* So, there are two vegetable elements with dissimilar attributes.

Types of Attributes

Type of Attribute	Description
String Type	Value is any literal string type. CDATA (character data) is a String Type. Meaning, any string type of markup characters can be considered as part of the attribute.
Tokenized Type	Characteristically, this type is more constrained. **ID** – identifies a unique element. **IDREF** – references an ID used to name another element. **IDREFS** – references all the IDs of an element. **ENTITY** – this indicates that the attribute represents external entities in the XML document. **ENTITIES** – the attribute is representing external entities in the XML document. **NMTOKEN** – this is similar to the CDATA, only with restrictions on the data that would be

	considered as part of the attribute. **NMTOKENS** – similar to the CDATA, but with restrictions on the data as part of the attribute.
Enumerated Type	This contains predefined values, out of which, one value has to be assigned. **Notation Type** – declares that a particular element shall be referenced to a NOTATION, to be declared somewhere in the document. **Enumeration** – it allows user to define a specific list of values that must match the attribute value.

Rules for Element Attribute

- The attribute name should not appear more than once in the same tag.

- There are no direct or indirect entity references to external entities in attribute values.

- The Document Type Definition (DTD) should reflect an attribute with the use of the Attribute-List-Declaration.

- The replacement text must not contain a less than sign (<).

XML Attribute Values Have to Be Quoted

In XML, the elements can have name/value pair attributes just like in HTML. However, the attributes in XML have to be quoted at all times. Consider the following sets of examples:

```
< note date = 12/25/2015 >
    <to> Jane </to>
    <from> John </from>
</note>
```

The example shown above is an incorrect way to use the date attribute. You have to keep in mind that quotes are necessary for attributes to work. In order to correct the mistake made in the above example, you have to edit your code and re-write it into something like this:

```
< note date = "12/25/2015" >
    <to> Jane </to>
    <from> John </from>
</note>
```

XML References

The references normally enable you to include additional markup or text in the XML document. These references should always begin with this symbol: "&", a reserved character that will have an ending symbol of ";".

Two References

Entity References – The entity reference consists of a name between the beginning and ending of the delimiters. For instance,

"&amp"amp" is the name that will be used. The name pertains to a predefined string of markups and tests.

Character References – These, on the other hand, seem to have a lot of stories to tell. Example is "A" which contains a hash mark, followed by a number. The number often refers to the Unicode code of a particular character. For instance, 65 refers to the alphabet.

XML Text

The *names* used for *XML-attributes* and *XML-elements* are case-sensitive, meaning the beginning and end should be written using the same case.

Prevent character encoding problems, by saving every XML file as a Unicode UTF 8 or UTF-16 file.

The whitespace characters, like tabs, blanks, and line breaks, between the elements and attributes should be ignored.

Some of the characters are reserved by the XML –syntax itself for direct use. This may work out fine but not for long. In order to use them, some replacement entities will have to be used, the choices are listed below:

Characters that are Not Allowed	Replacement Entity	Description
<	&lt;	Less than

>	>	Greater than
&	&	Ampersand
'	'	Apostrophe
"	"	Quotation mark

Chapter 4 XML Documents

The basic unit of XML information, the XML document, consists of elements and markups in an organized package, and has a variety of data. Examples of XML documents are a database of numbers, a mathematical equation, and numbers that represent molecular structure.

Example

A simple XML document looks like this:

```
<?xml version="1.0"?>  ⎫ ─────────────→     Document
Prolog                 ⎭

<contact-info>

<name>Elaine Cooper</name>       ⎫
<company>Science Joint</company> ⎬─────→     Document
Element                          ⎭

<phone>(555) 115-8452</phone>

</contact-info>
```

Parts of an XML Document

Document Prolog – It is found at the top of the document just before the root element. It contains the *XML declaration* and the *document type declaration*. (You'll learn more about this when XML declaration is discussed in the next chapter.)

Document Elements Section – The document elements are the main building blocks of XML. These elements divide the document into sections, each are serving their own purpose. You are allowed to separate an XML document into different sections so rendering is easier. Doing so would also allow other search engines to take a tab for it. These elements can be containers , with a combination of elements and text.

Types of Document

A document with a correct syntax is described as *well formed*. Valid documents have to conform to document type definitions. The rules that define the legal attributes and elements for the documents in XML are known as XML Schemas or Document Type Definitions (DTD). The DTD is the original Document Type Definition and the XML Schema is an XML-based alternative to it.

All XML documents have to have a root element. Their elements should have a closing tag and should be nested properly. Their attribute values should be quoted and their tags should match since they are case sensitive. Consider the following example of a well formed XML document:

```
<?xml version = "1.0" encoding = "UTF – 8"?>
<note>
<to> John </to>
<from> Jane </from>
<heading> Memo </heading>
<body> Do not forget the meeting scheduled for tomorrow afternoon.
</body>
</note>
```

Using the DTD or Schema

Anyone can use a standard DTD to interchange data. Your application can make use of it for data verification purposes. In other words, you can use DTD to find out if the data you obtained from external sources are valid. In addition, you can use DTD to check and verify your own data.

Its main purpose is to define the structure of a document in XML. It uses a list of legal elements to define such structure. To help you understand this further, consider the following example:

```
<! DOCTYPE memo
[
<! ELEMENT memo (to, from, heading, body)>
<! ELEMENT to (#PCDATA)>
<! ELEMENT from (#PCDATA)>
<! ELEMENT heading (#PCDATA)>
<! ELEMENT body (#PCDATA)>
]>
```

In the example given above, #PCDATA refers to parse-able text data. Parsed Character Data (PCDATA) is actually a data definition that came from the Standard Generalized Markup Language (SGML). It is also used in Extensible Markup Language Document Type Definition for designating mixed content elements in XML.

Still referring to the example shown above, DTD is interpreted as follows:

- !DOCTYPE memo states that the root element of the XML document is memo.

- !ELEMENT memo states that the memo element has to have four elements, which are to, from, heading, and body.

- !ELEMENT to states that the to element belongs under the #PCDATA type.

- !ELEMENT from states that the from element belongs under the #PCDATA type.

- !ELEMENT heading states that the heading element belongs under the #PCDATA type.

- !ELEMENT body states that the body element belongs under the #PCDATA type.

You can also use a doctype declaration to define character strings and special characters. Remember that an entity has to include an ampersand (&), a semicolon (;), and an entity name.

Then again, a DTD or Schema is not required in XML. Thus, you may only be wasting your time if you create a DTD when you work with small files or experiment with XML.

If you are developing an application, you must wait until you get a stable specification before you add a definition to the document. Otherwise, you may receive validation errors that may cause your software to stop working.

Chapter 5 The XML Declaration

The XML declaration consists of details put in order by an XML processor to break down and analyze the XML document. This is optional, however, when it is utilized; it has to appear in the first line of the XML document.

Syntax

<?xml

    version="version_number"

    encoding="encoding_declaration"

    standalone="standalone_status"

?>

The above is a syntax showing XML declaration.

Each of the parameters have their own name, equal sign (=), and value inside a quote. This table above shows the detailed XML syntax parameters:

Parameter	Parameter_value	Parameter_description
Version	1.0	The XML standard version supposed to be used.
Encoding	UTF-8, UTF 16, ISO-8859-1 to ISO-8859-9, ISO 10646-USC-2, ISO 10646-USC-4,	Defines the character encoding as used in the content. The default encoding used is UTF-8.

	ISO-2022-JP, EUC-JP, JIS	
Standalone	yes or no	It alerts the parser if the document relies on information from an external source, like the external document type definition or DTD, for its contents. *No* is the default value. When you set it to *yes,* it indicates that there are no declarations needed for parsing the XML document.

Rules to Keep in Mind

- If there is XML declaration in the XML, it has to be positioned as the first line in the XML document.

- The XML declaration should contain the version number attribute.

- Parameter values and names are case-sensitive.

- Names should always be in lower case.

- The parameter name should be in proper order: version, encoding, standalone.

- You can use either the single or double quotes.

- XML declaration does not contain a closing tag, like </?xml>

- The XML declaration should always be in lowercase, except when encoding declarations.

- If there are elements, entities, or attributes in the XML document that are defined or referenced in an external DTD, there should be *standalone = "no"*.

XML Declaration Example

With all the parameters defined:

<?xml> version='1.0' encoding='iso-8859-1' standalone='no'

Chapter 6 XML Comments and Character Entities

XML comments are like the HTML comments. They are added as notes to help understand the purpose of a particular XML code. They can be used to include related information, terms, and links. However, they can only be seen in the source code, and not in the XML code.

Syntax

<!-------Your comment----->

An XML comment always begins with <!—and ends with -->. Notes can be added as comments in between the characters. It is not advisable to nest one comment inside another.

Example

<?xml version="1.0" encoding="UTF-8" ?>

<!---Test scores are uploaded by grade---->

<class_list>

    <student>

    <name>Lilly</name>

```
<grade>B+</grade>

</student>
```

```
</class_list>
```

XML Character Entities

An XML entity is the root of the entity tree and the starting-point for the XML processor. It is the placeholder in XML. Entities can be acknowledged being in the document prolog or the DTD. There are symbols that are to be used exclusively for entities that cannot be used as content in the XML code; this is true for both XML and HTML. For instance, < and > are used for the opening and closing tags. The character entities are used to make these special characters visible.

There are some special characters and symbols that are not directly available via a computer keyboard. Character entities are used to display these special characters.

Types of Character Entities

Predefined Character Entities

These are introduced to prevent ambiguity when some symbols are used. For example, there is ambiguity when the symbols (<) and (>) are used with the angle tag (<>). The character entities are used to delimit tags. Here are specifications of pre-defined character entities.

The following can be used to express the characters without resulting in ambiguity.

- Greater than: &gt

- Less than: <

- Ampersand: &

- Single quote: '

- Double quote: "

Numerical Character Entities

This type uses number reference to define a character entity. It can either be in hexadecimal or decimal format. There are thousands of numeric references known to man and they are not easy to remember.

The numeric reference is a number in the Unicode character set. This is the syntax for decimal number reference:

&# decimal number ;

This is the syntax for hexadecimal reference:

&#x Hexadecimal number ;

This table shows some of the commonly used predefined character entities and their numeric values:

Entity name	Character	Decimal reference	Hexadecimal reference
Quot	"	&#34;	&#x22;
Amp	&	&#38;	&#x26;
Apos	'	&#39;	&#x27;
Lt	<	&#60;	&#x3C;
Gt	>	&#62;	&#x3E;

Named Character References

Remembering all the numeric characters would be too hard; hence, the most preferred by users is the named character entity. Here are some examples:

- *Acute* refers to the capital Á character with acute accent.

- *Ugrave* is the name given to the small ù with grave accent.

ιpter 7 CDATA Sections and Whitespaces

CDATA is Character Data; it is refers to blocks of text not parsed by the assigned parser, but are still recognized as markup. Keep in mind that CDATA sections and CDATA attributes are not related. CDATA attributes are strings and allow any text.

In an XML document, the CDATA section commands the parser to ignore the markup characters. Take a look at source code listings in XML documents. They may have characters that the parser would normally consider as markup, such as & and <. In order for these characters to be passed onto the application, a CDATA section is necessary. Consider the following example:

```
<! [CDATA [
*x = &y;
A = ( j <= 5 );
] ] >
```

Between the beginning and the end of the section showed above, all of the character data are directly passed onto the application without any interpretation. Entity references, elements, processing instructions, and comments are not recognized and whatever character comprises them is passed literally onto the application. *]] >* is the only string that can never occur in a CDATA section.

Some predefined entities, like *<* and *>* need typing and are quite hard to read in the markup, this is where CDATA section is needed. CDATA section, when used, will command the parser that a particular section of the XML document has no markup and should be treated as regular text.

Syntax

```
<![CDATA[
```

characters with markup

]]>

This syntax has three sections:

- **CDATA Start Section** – it should always begin with the 9-letter delimiter <![CDATA[

- **CDATA End Section** – it usually ends with]]> delimeter.

- **CDATA Section** – the characters between the start and end sections are referred to as characters. They are not recognized as markups. It may contain some markup characters but they are often neglected by the XML processor.

Example

This is a markup code. The characters inside the CDAT are ignored by the parser.

<script>

<![CDATA[

Ahoy! You're in SeaShack

]] >

</script >

Rules

- CDATA is not supposed to contain the string *"]]>* anywhere in the document.

- CDATA section does not allow nesting.

The XML Whitespaces

A whitespace is a collection of newlines, tabs, and of course, spaces. They make the XML document easy to read.

The XML document has 2 types of white spaces:

- Significant Whitespace
- Insignificant Whitespace

Significant Whitespaces

This will occur within the element that contain the text and the markup that are present together.

Examples

<name>NelDelgado</name>

Or

Nel Delgado

Take note of the difference between the spaces of each element. Any program that is reading this type of element in an XML file should maintain the recognition.

Insignificant Whitespace

This is the space that only allows element content.

<address.category="work">

Or

<address....category="..work">

These samples are the same. The dots represent the space. The space between *address* and *category* on the above sample may actually be significant.

xml:space, a special attribute, can be attached to a particular element. The addition would indicate that the whitespace should not be removed for the particular element. This can be set as either *default* or *preserve*.

<!ATTLIST address xml:space (default|preserve) 'preserve'>

- The value *default* allows that the default whitespace processing modes of a particular application to be accepted for this particular element.

- The value *preserve* commands the application to preserve all the whitespaces.

Chapter 8 XML Processing and XM Encoding

Processing instructions allow the documents to contain instructions for every application. These are not part of the character data of the XML document, but they have to pass through the application.

PIs allows you to pass information to all the applications. They can appear anywhere in the document. They may also appear in the prolog, which includes the DTD or document type definition, after the document, or as textual content.

Syntax

<?target instructions?>

- The *target* recognizes the application from which the instruction originates.

- The *instruction* is a character that is used to describe the information that the application needs to process.

A processing instruction begins in a special tag <? and ends with ?>. When the string ?> is encountered, the processing abruptly ends.

Example

Though PIs are not often used, they are used to link an XML document to a style sheet. This is what it looks like:

<?xml-stylesheet href="businessforms.css" type="text/css"?>

The **target** is the *xml-stylesheet.href="businessforms.css"*

type=text/css are the instructions that the target application will have to process for the XML document.

With this instruction, the browser will recognize the target by initiating that the XML document should be transformed before begin shown. Notice that the 1st attribute recognizes the type of XSL transform, while the 2nd attribute indicates its location.

Rules

A processing instruction contains data except for the combination *?>*, which is interpreted as a closing delimeter.

Examples

    <?welcome to pg=55 of business hub?>

Or this:

    <?hello?>

XML Encoding

The process of encoding converts Unicode characters into binary. The moment the XML processor reads a specific XML document, it immediately encodes the document according to the type of encoding that is needed.

Types of Encoding

There are two types of encoding: UTF-8 and UTF-16. *UTF* means *USC Transformational Format; USC* is *Universal Character Set.* Numbers 8 and 16 indicate the bits used to represent the characters. UTF-8 is 1 byte, while UTF-16 is 2 bytes. If an XML document has no encoding information, the default set is UTF-8.

Syntax

The type of encoding has to be indicated in the prolog section of the XML document itself.

UTF-8 syntax:

    <?xml version="1.0" encoding="UTF-8" standalone="no" ?>

UTF-16 syntax:

    <?xml version="1.0" encoding="UTF-16" standalone="no" ?>

Example

```
<?xml version="1.0" encoding="UTF-8" standalone="no" ?>

<contact-info>

    <name>Dunny Bobbins</name>

    <company>Real Realtors</company>

    <phone>(553) 512-1123</phone>

</contact-info>
```

This sample indicates the use of UTF-8 encoding, meaning 8-bit characters should be used. Files encoded using UTF-8 is smaller in size than those used in UTF-16.

Chapter 9 XML Validation

The validation process is needed in order to know if the contents of the document match the elements, DTD, and/or attributes. Validation is also used to determine whether the document complies with the restrictions indicated in it.

Validation is done by the XML parser in 2 ways: well-formed XML document or valid XML document.

Well-formed XML Document

A document should adhere to the following rules to become well-formed:

- A DTD XML file should not contain the following character entities: *amp (&), lt (<), gt (>), quot (double quote), and apos (single quote.*

- Proper tag order should be followed; for instance the inner tag should be closed even before closing the outer tag.

- All tags should contain a closing tag, or it has to have a self-ending tag.

- The start tag should contain only 1 attribute in your extra tag.

- *Amp(&), lt(<), gt (>), quot(double quote),* and *apos(single quote)* entities other these mentioned should be declared.

Example

```
<?xml version="1.0" encoding="UTF-8" standalone="yes" ?>

<!DOCTYPE address
[
    <!ELEMENT address (name,company,phone)>

    <!ELEMENT name (#PCDATA)>

    <!ELEMENT company (#PCDATA)>

    <!ELEMENT phone (#PCDATA)>

]>

<address>

    <name>Dunny Bobbins</name>

    <company>Real Realtors</company>

    <phone>(333) 115-7785</phone>

</address>
```

This is well-formed because of the following:

- The type of document is indicated (it is in element type).

- It has a root element, the address.

- Self-explanatory tags enclose each of the child elements.

- Order of the tags are well-maintained.

Valid Document

A well-formed XML document with Document Type Declaration or DTD, is a valid XML document. The vocabulary and validity of the structure of XML documents are checked against the grammatical rules of the appropriate XML language.

Syntax

Basic syntax:

```
<!DOCTYPE element DTD identifier
```

The DTD identifier is used for the document type definition. It may be the path in your system or the URL link. If it is pointing to an external path, it is referred to as the External Subset.

Internal DTD

The elements are within the XML files. To refer to an internal DTD, the standalone attribute in the XML declaration should be set to *yes*.

Syntax

<!DOCTYPE root-element [element-declarations]>

Example

<?xml version="1.0" encoding="UTF-8" standalone="yes" ?>

<!DOCTYPE address [

    <!ELEMENT address (name,company,phone)>

    <!ELEMENT name (#PCDATA)>

    <!ELEMENT company (#PCDATA)>

    <!ELEMENT phone (#PCDATA)>
]>

<address>

<name>Dunny Bobbins</name>

<company>Real Realtors</company>

<phone>(088) 559-4456</phone>

</address>

Rules

- The document type declaration should always be at the beginning of the document.

- Element declarations should always begin with an exclamation mark.

- The *name* indicated in the document type declaration should match the *element type* of the root element.

External DTD

The DTD elements are declared outside the XML file. The standalone attribute has to be set to *no* to refer to the external DTD.

Syntax

<!DOCTYPE root-element SYSTEM "file-name">

Example

```
<?xml version="1.0" encoding="UTF-8" standalone="no" ?>

<!DOCTYPE address SYSTEM "address.dtd">

<address>

    <name>Dunny Bobbins</name>

    <company>Real Realtors</company>

    <phone>(077) 554-4453</phone>

</address>
```

The content of address.dtd looks like this:

```
<!ELEMENT address (name,company,phone)>

<!ELEMENT name (#PCDATA)>

<!ELEMENT company (#PCDATA)>
```

<!ELEMENT phone (#PCDATA)>

Types of External DTD

- System Identifiers – this allows you to specify the location of the external file.

  <!DOCTYPE name SYSTEM "address.dtd" [...]>

- Public Identifiers – provides mechanisms to locate DTD resources.

<!DOCTYPE name PUBLIC "-//Beginning XML//DTD Address Example//EN">

Chapter 10 XML Schemas

XML Schema is more commonly referred to as XML Schema Definition or XSD. It can be used to validate the structure and content, and at the same time describe the content of the XML data.

Syntax

```
<xs:schema
xmlns:xs="http://www.business.com/2012/XMLSchema">
```

Example

```
<?xml version="1.0" encoding="UTF-8"?>


<xs:schema
xmlns:xs="http://www.business.com/2012/XMLSchema">


<xs:element name="contact">


    <xs:complexType>


        <xs:sequence>


            <xs:element name="name" type="xs:string" />
```

```
<xs:element name="company" type="xs:string" />

<xs:element name="phone" type="xs:int" />

</xs:sequence>

</xs:complexType>

</xs:element>

</xs:schema>
```

Definition Types

- Simple Type – utilized in the context of the text.

  ```
  <xs:element name="phone_number" type="xs:int" />
  ```

- Complex Type – this is a container for other element definitions.

  ```
  <xs:element name="Address">

  <xs:complexType>

  <xs:sequence>
  ```

```
        <xs:element   name="name"   type="xs:string"
/>

        <xs:element                name="company"
type="xs:string" />

        <xs:element name="phone" type="xs:int" />

    </xs:sequence>

  </xs:complexType>

</xs:element>
```

- Global Types – can be defined in a single type document.

```
<xs:element name="AddressType">

    <xs:complexType>

        <xs:sequence>

            <xs:element              name="name"
type="xs:string" />
```

```
            <xs:element            name="company"
type="xs:string" />
    </xs:sequence>


    </xs:complexType>


</xs:element>
```

Chapter 11 Tags and Elements

XML tags are one of the most vital parts of XML. They are practically the foundation of this language. They define the scopes of elements, declare settings necessary for parsing environments, insert special instructions, and insert comments. XML tags are categorized into the following:

Start Tag

A start tag marks the start of all non-empty XML elements. For example:

<address>

Empty Tag

In between the start tag and the end tag, there is a text and it is called the *content*. If an element does not have a *content*, it is described as *empty*. Empty elements are generally represented in a couple of ways, which are as follows:

1. An end tag immediately follows a start tag, such as:
   <hr> </hr>

2. A complete empty element tag, such as:
   <hr />

Empty element tags can be used for elements that do not have any content.

End Tag

The end tag is necessary in an element if it has a start tag. For example:

</address>

Take note that the end tag has a solidus (/) prior to the name of the element.

Rules for Using Tags in XML

- Unlike other languages, XML is actually case sensitive. This means that you have to be careful when using uppercase and lowercase characters. Keep in mind that the tags in XML should either be all uppercase or all lowercase. A single mistake can have undesirable results, which is why it is recommended that you review your codes before you enter or finalize them. Take a look at the following example of a wrong syntax used in a line code:

<address> </Address>

As you can see, the first letter in the end tag is capitalized while the rest of the letters are not. Because there is a case difference in both of the tags, XML treats it as an erroneous syntax. In order to fix this error, you need to use the same case in both your start tag and end tag. This is the correct syntax:

<address> </address>

- Another rule for using tags in XML that you have to keep in mind is that the tags should be closed in the right order. For instance, if a tag is opened in another element, it has to be closed before the external element is closed. Take a look at the following example of this rule:

```
<external_element>
<internal_element>
The tag is closed before the external_element
</internal_element>
</external_element>
```

59

Naming Rules in XML

You should take not that all elements in XML should follow these rules:

- The element names are case sensitive. So if you want to use 'phone', you have to make sure that you are consistent in your uppercase and lowercase characters. Take note that 'phone', 'PHONE', and 'Phone' are all considered as different names in XML.
- The start tag and the end tag of the element has to be identical or exactly the same.
- The element names have to begin with either an underscore or a letter.
- The element names cannot begin with 'xml', 'Xml', or 'XML'. Basically, you cannot use the word 'xml' at the beginning of your element no matter what form you use. It will not matter if you use lowercase letters, uppercase letters, or a combination of both.
- The element names are allowed to have periods, underscores, hyphens, digits, and letters. They are allowed to contain alphanumeric characters. However, the only punctuation marks they can contain are the period (.), hyphen (-), and underscore (_).
- The element names are not allowed to have spaces.
- The container can contain elements or texts.

In XML, you are allowed to use any name you want, with the exception of 'xml'.

Elements in XML

The elements in XML may be defined as the building blocks of XML. These elements can act as containers that hold text, attributes, elements, media objects, and even a combination of all these functions. Every document has one or more elements whose scopes are delimited by the start tag and the end tag. For empty elements, on the other hand, the scopes are delimited by the empty element tag.

Syntax

When writing the syntax in XML, you should follow this format:

```
<element-name attribute1 attribute2>
Whatever your content is
</element-name>
```

Referring to the example given above, element-name is the name of the element while attribute 1 and attribute2 are the attributes of the element which are divided by white spaces. The *attribute* defines the property of the element. It works by associating the name with its corresponding value, which is typically a string of characters. When writing the attribute, you have to write it as follows:

name = "value"

When writing the name of your element, see to it that the name you use in the start tag matches the name you use in the end tag. In addition, the *name* should be followed by an equal (=) sign as well as a string value inside single quotes (' ') or double quotes (" ").

Empty Element

As you have learned in a previous lesson, an empty element is an element that does not have any content. When writing its syntax, you have to follow the following format:

```
<name attribute1 attribute2... />
```

If you are creating a document and you have to use a variety of elements, you can follow this format:

```
<?xml version = "1.0"?>
<contact-information>
<address category = "home">
<name> Wendy Dawn </name>
```

61

```
<office> My Office </office>
<phone> (632) 246-1234 </phone>
<address/>
</contact-information>
```

Chapter 12 Tree Structure

Tree Structure in XML

When creating documents in XML, see to it that they are descriptive. You can use a tree structure, also known as the XML Tree, to include details in your document. This tree structure is very important in a program. Without them, it will be difficult for you to describe your documents.

Basically, a tree structure has root elements or parent elements and child elements. Through a tree structure, you will be able to identify all the branches and the sub-branches included in your program. You will be able to see everything from the root down to the branches and leaf nodes. The parsing actually begins at the root and then it moves downward to the first branch, leaf nodes, and so on and so forth.

Consider the following example of a simple tree structure in XML:

```
<?xml version = "1.0"?>
<Business>
<Member>
<FirstName> Wendy </FirstName>
<LastName> Dawn </LastName>
<PhoneNumber> 1234567 </PhoneNumber>
<Email> wendydawn@eph.com </Email>
<Address>
<State> California </State>
<City> Sacramento </City>
<ZipCode> 94203 </ZipCode>
</Address>
</Member>
</Business>
```

Using the document given above, here is the tree structure that corresponds to it:

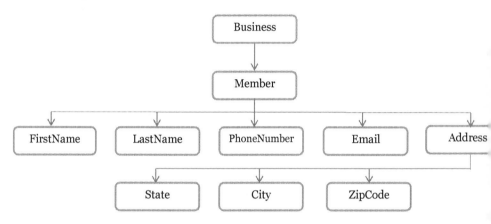

In the diagram shown above, a root element called <business> is present. Within that element, another element, which is called <member> is found. In this element, there are branches connected to it. These branches are <FirstName>, <LastName>, <PhoneNumber>, <Email>, and <Address>. Conversely, there are also sub-branches connected to the element <Address>, and these are <State>, <City>, and <ZipCode>.

Chapter 13 Document Object Model, Namespaces, and Databases

The Document Object Model (DOM) is, in fact, the foundation of XML. All documents created in XML consist of a hierarchy of informative units known as *nodes*. The Document Object Model is a way to describe nodes and their respective relationships. It is a collection of information pieces or nodes that are organized according to their hierarchy, which allows you to navigate through the tree in search of a particular information. Since it is based on an information hierarchy, it is classified as *tree based*.

The Document Object Model in XML also offers an API that lets you add, move, remove, or edit nodes in your tree at any point you like. This is to allow you to make your application. Take a look at the following example. It parses a document into a Document Object Model object and extracts certain information from it using JavaScript.

```
<!DOCTYPE html>
<html>
<body>
<h1> Example of a Document Object Model </h1>
<div>
<b> Business </b> <span id = "business"> </span> <br>
<b> Member </b> <span id = "member"> </span> <br>
<b> Number </b> <span id = "number"> </span>
</div>
```

Namespaces in XML

Namespaces are sets of unique names in XML. A namespace is basically a mechanism wherein the element and the attribute name are allowed to be assigned to a group. The Uniform Resource Identifier (URI) identifies the namespace.

Namespace Declaration

Namespaces are declared with the use of reserved attributes. Keep in mind that the attribute name has to either start with *xmlns:* or be *xmlns*. Consider the following example:

<element xmlns:name = "URL">

Namespace Syntax

As mentioned earlier, the namespace has to start with the keyword *xmlns*. Using the example given above, URL is your Namespace identifier while name is your Namespace prefix.

The Namespace only affects a certain area in a document. The element that contains the declaration as well as every one of its descendants are included in the scope of the Namespace. Take a look at the following example:

<?xml version = "1.0" encoding = "UTF-8"?>
<cont : contact xmlns:cont = www.sampleprograms.net/profile>
<cont : company> Sample Programs </cont : company>
<cont : name> John Doe </cont : name>
<cont : phone> (012) 246-1234 </cont : phone>
</cont : contact>

Using the example shown above, *cont* serves as your Namespace prefix while www.sampleprograms.net/profile serves as your Namespace identifier or URI. With this being said, you can say that the attribute names and the element names with the prefix *cont*, including your contact element, are classified under the namespace www.sampleprograms.net/profile.

Databases in XML

The Database is used for storing large amounts of information in XML format. Because XML is increasing in popularity in numerous fields, it has been required to have a secured place for storing documents. Thus, the data stored in databases are queried through *XQuery*. Then, they are serialized and finally exported into the preferred format.

Types of Databases in XML

In XML, there are two primary types of databases: Native XML or NXD and XML-enabled. The Native XML Database is not based on the table format. Instead, it is based on the container. It is capable of storing large amounts of data and documents in XML. In addition, it is queried by XPath-expressions. More programmers actually prefer the Native XML Database to the XML-Enabled Database due to its better ability to query, maintain, and store the document in XML. Because of this, the Native XML Database is considered to be much more advantageous than the XML-Enabled Database.

On the other hand, the XML-Enabled Database is simply an extension for converting documents in XML. It is a relational database in which the data are stored in tables that consist of columns and rows. These tables contain sets of records that consist of fields. Take a look at the following example that demonstrates the database in XML.

```
<?xml version = "1.0"?>
<contact-information>
<contact1>
<company> Sample Company </company>
<name> Jane Doe </name>
<phone> (012) 246-1234 </phone>
</contact1>
<contact2>
<company> Sample Company </company>
<name> John Doe </name>
<phone> (012) 123-5678 </phone>
</contact2>
</contact-information>
```

If you run the code shown above, you will get an output that consists of a table of contacts. You will see a record of contact information, which also contains three entities. These entities are the company, name, and phone of contact1 and contact2.

Chapter 14 XML Viewers and Editors

In XML, there are a variety of methods you can use to view documents. For instance, you can view a document using any browser or a simple text editor. Majority of browsers actually support XML, so you do not have to worry about your browser not supporting it. You can open your files in XML simply by double clicking on them. However, this only works if your document is a local file. If your file is found on the server, you have to type in the URL path in your address bar the same way you do when you open your other files in your browser. Do not forget to save your files with a ".xml" extension.

To help you understand the methods used for viewing files in XML, consider the following example.

```
<?xml version = "1.0"?>
<contact-information>
<company> Sample Programs </company>
<name> Juan dela Cruz </name>
<phone> (012) 123-4321 </phone>
</contact-information>
```

Text Editors in XML

You can actually use any text editor you want. You can use Textpad, TextEdit, or Notepad to view and create documents in XML.

Using Google Chrome

Google Chrome is one of the major browsers that support XML. So if you are using this browser, you are in luck. You can easily open your XML code.

Using Mozilla Firefox

Mozilla Firefox also supports XM, but first, you have to open your code in Google Chrome. To do this, you have to double click on your file. You will then see your code displayed in colorful text. This is great because you will be able to read your code more easily. At the left portion of the element, you will see the plus (+) sign and the minus (-) sign. If you click on the plus (+) sign, your code lines will expand. On the other hand, if you click on the minus (-) sign, your code will be hidden.

Document Errors in XML

If you notice that your code has certain tags missing, you may have an error. If so, you will see a message that tells you about the error that you have. Take a look at the following example:

```
<?xml version = "1.0"?>
<contact-information>
<company> Sample Company </company>
<name> Jane Doe </name>
<phone> (045) 123-5678 </phone>
</cntact-information>
```

If you open the above given code in Google Chrome, you will receive an error message. As you can see, the start tag <contact-information> and the end tag </cntact-information> do not match.

Editors in XML

An editor is a markup language editor. Documents in XML can be created and edited with the use of existing editors. For instance, you can use Wordpad, Notepad, or any other text editor on your computer. You can even use a professional editor online if you want to download. Online editors usually have more powerful editing features. They automatically close tags that are left open and they strictly check syntax. They highlight syntax with color for easier readability as well as provide automatic verification of documents against schemas and DTDs. They are also helpful in writing valid codes in XML.

Open Source Editors in XML

In XML, you can choose from a variety of editors. The available open source editors include the following:

Xerlin. It is an open source editor developed for the Java 2 platform, which was released under the Apache license. Since it is a Java based modelling application, it can be used to create and edit files in XML much more easily.

Content Assembly Mechanism (CAM). It is an editor tool that features XML + JSON + SQL Open-XDX which is sponsored by Oracle.

Chapter 15 Parsers and Processors in XML

In XML, a parser is a package or software library that provides an interface for a client application to work with a document. It checks the document and verifies if it has the right format. It can also validate the documents. Today, most browsers include built-in parsers for XML, so you do not have to worry about your browser not supporting it. It is unusual for major browsers to not have a built-in parser.

To help you understand parsers better, here is a diagram that demonstrates how a parser interacts with a document in XML:

The primary goal of the parser is to turn XML into a code that is readable and understandable. In order to make the process of parsing easier, certain commercial products can be used. These products are available for breaking down XML documents and yielding more reliable results. The following are some of the most commonly used parsers:

Microsoft Core XML Services (MSXML). It is the standard set of XML tools available in Microsoft. It includes a parser.

Java built-in parser. It is the parser solely available in the Java library. This library is developed in a way that a user can replace such built-in parser with an external implementation, such as Saxon or Xerces from Apache.

Xerces. It is developed by the Apache Software Foundation, which is a well-known open source. It is also implemented in Java.

Saxon. It offers tool for the purpose of parsing, querying, and transforming XML.

System.Xml.XmlDocument. It is a class that is part of the .NET library. This library contains numerous classes that are related to working with XML.

Processors in XML

Processing the XML is whenever a software program reads a document and then takes the necessary action. A program that has the ability to process and read documents in XML is referred to as an *XML processor*. The XML processor reads the file and transforms it into in-memory structures that are accessible to the other parts of the program. The most vital processor reads the documents and turns them into internal representations that the other subroutines or programs can use. This is known as the *parser*. It is actually a crucial component in the processing programs of XML.

Types of Processors

The processors are mainly classified into two types, which are validating and non-validating. These types depend on whether or not the processors check the documents for validity. The processors that discover validity errors should report such errors. Nevertheless, they may continue or resume with their normal processing.

Some of the validating parsers include: xml4c (C++, IBM), xml4j (Java, IBM), MSXML (Java, Microsoft), TclXML (TCL), XML :: Parser (Perl), xmlproc (Phyton), and Java Project X (Java, Sun).

Some of the non-validating parsers include: OpenXML (Java), xp (Java), Lark (Java), AElfred (Java), XParse (JavaScript), expat (C), and xmllib (Phyton).

Processing Instructions in XML

The processor is about processing instructions. Processing Instructions are actually special tags that include instructions to the software on how to use the document. If you are a beginner, you may think that Processing Instructions are quite complicated. However, Processing Instructions are not used very often.

Importance of Processing Instructions

If you are used to using HTML, you have probably noticed that it does not have Processing Instructions. Whenever you have to send out instructions to the software, you need to misuse the comment tag. A classical example of this misuse is the Server Side Includes (SSI). Although a misuse, it is for a good purpose. Take a look at the following example of an SSI that includes a file.

```
<!--- #include virtual = "samplefile.txt" -->
```

Yes, this may seem like a smart and practical idea. However, you have to keep in mind that it is still a misuse of the comment tag. The comment tag has a specific purpose and that is to include comments in the program. It is not designed to be used this way. Nonetheless, if your HTML page has an *shtml* file extension, the Web server will search for SSI and process it before your page is sent to your browser.

Another way to serve CSS and optimized markup for the Internet Explorer browser more easily is to use *conditional comments*. Take a look at the following example:

```
<!—(if IE 6)>
<link rel = "stylesheet" type = "text/css" href = ie6only.css>
<! (endif) -->
```

Again, this is another way to use a comment tag. However, it is still a misuse because you are not using the comment tag to insert comments in the program.

Because of the misuse of the comment tag for other purposes, developers have found a way to beat these limitations in the XML. They have acknowledged that there are special needs that may not be possible to foresee. These special needs are actually much more likely to occur in XML than in HTML because XML is a meta markup language.

In addition, the Processing Instructions tag was developed in order to protect the comment tag against misuse. It was also developed to offer a flexible universal mechanism for every type of special need that is not immediately solved by attributes and elements.

Processing Instructions

Processing Instructions make it possible for documents to have instructions for applications. They are, however, not part of the character data of these documents. They also have to be passed through to the applications.

It is compulsory for every processor to ignore the meaning of the Processing Instructions since they do not know what they stand for anyway. Nevertheless, the process has to pass the content and name of the Processing Instruction onto the applications.

Take a look at the following XML spec:

PI : : = '<?' PITarget (S (Char* - (Char* '?>' Char*))) ? '?>'

PITarget : : = Name – (('X' | 'X') ('M' | 'm') ('L' | 'l'))

The PI Target or the name that follows the first question mark is actually the name of the Processing Instruction. A space has to be placed after it. The rest of the Processing Instruction, including the last question mark, is a string value or the content. The letters *xml* are reserved, as you have learned in a previous chapter. Thus, it should not be used to begin a user-defined Processing Instruction name. Likewise, the content should not include the characters *?>*.

As you can see, the content of the Processing Instruction is only a string value. Nonetheless, it is a common practice to create content that appears to be pseudo-attributes. Take a look at the following example:

<? xml – stylesheet href = "sample.css" type = "text/css" ?>

Aside from this, you may also write "abc1234567" or "Processing Instructions are quite unusual but you can eventually get used to using them." These examples are considered legal content in XML.

Common Uses of Processing Instructions

Processing Instructions are not used very often, except in certain instances. They are, in fact, the official method for XML documents to be linked to stylesheets. Microsoft makes use of Processing Instructions in Microsoft Office 2003. This is so the user can easily identify Microsoft Excel and Microsoft Word documents when saving them as XML.

XML Stylesheet

In 1999, using Processing Instructions to link stylesheets to XML documents has been a standard practice.

Processing Instructions in Microsoft Office 2003

Ever since the development of the Microsoft Office 2003, Processing Instructions have become more popular amongst users. Both Word and Excel can now save in their very own xml formats with the use of an *xml* file extension. Then again, this has proven to be an inefficient method because a lot of other applications also use the same extension.

Because of this, Microsoft has used Processing Instructions for identification. This is so XML files can be signaled to Windows Explorer and Internet Explorer either as Excel or Word documents.

If you are using Microsoft Word 2003, the Processing Instruction found after the XML declaration appears as follows:

<? mso-application progid = "Word.Document" ?>

If you are using Microsoft Excel 2003, the Processing Instruction found after the XML declaration appears as follows:

<? mso-application progid = "Excel.Sheet" ?>

Microsoft Office 2007 makes use of a zip file format for PowerPoint (pptx), Word (docx), and Excel (xlsx). Every zipped document has several media files, XML files, and other files. If you are using Microsoft Office 2007, there is no more need for you to use Processing Instructions because the file extensions available are already enough. However, if you want to save your file in the 2003 XML format and you are using Microsoft Office 2007, Processing Instructions may be used.

Processing Instructions for Nearly Everything

Processing Instructions are highly versatile. In fact, they can be used to do a variety of things, such as indicating line breaks in markups and determining the words that do not have to be spell checked among others.

In order for you to understand Processing Instructions better, consider the following example. Here, you will learn about the diversity of Processing Instructions. You will find out how they can solve nearly every problem. For instance, if you have a project in XML, you can use Processing Instructions to annotate your documents that are still in process.

<? TeamExample member = "Wendy" date = "2015-11-04" comment = "I believe that the attributes given in the product element are not of particular importance and therefore can be eliminated." ?>

If you used comment tags, you may have a hard time differentiating the actual comments from the other elements in your document. So in order for you to solve such problem, you can use Processing Instructions. There is no more need for you to declare them in your schema. You can easily differentiate them from actual comments as well as delete them if necessary.

Comments only have content. Processing Instructions, on the other hand, have both content and a name. For instance, you can use *the processing-instruction ( )* node test to match all Processing Instructions in XPath. Nonetheless, you can also search for Processing Instructions by name and have their content returned. In order for that to happen, you need to do the following:

processing-instruction ( ) [name ( ) = "TeamExample"]

Keep in mind that the content is simply a long string and that the pseudo values of pseudo attributes may be analyzed with the use of Regular Expressions.

When Should You Use Processing Instructions?

Ideally, you should use Processing Instructions when you no longer have any choice. In other words, you should consider them as your last resort. As much as possible, you should refrain from using them. If you use them when it is not necessary, they will only be ignored. This is especially true if the software program does not understand what they stand for. Take note that even professional developers need to know what they mean before they can use them. Processing Instructions are not easy to grasp unlike the xml-stylesheet Processing Instructors and the Processing Instructors found in Microsoft Office 2003.

XML Declarations Are Not Processing Instructions

A lot of people have this misconception that XML declarations are Processing Instructions or Special Processing Instructions. However, you should know that this is far from the truth. XML declarations and Processing Instructions are actually very different.

Even though an xml declaration looks and acts like a Processing Instruction, its function is different. An xml processor is aware of the xml declaration and its content. In fact, it knows it so well that it can quickly return an error message in case it finds something wrong with it.

With Processing Instructions, things are different. They are actually the exact opposite. The xml processor ignores the Processing Instructions, but passes their name and content onto the application.

The World Wide Web Consortium (W3C), an international community that creates open standards to ensure the long term growth of the Web, recommends the Extensive Stylesheet Language Transformations (XSLT) and the XML Path Language (XPath) for transforming information marked up in XML from a certain vocabulary to another.

These two offer an excellent implementation of a tree-oriented transformation language. They transmute XML instances that use a single vocabulary into plain text, legacy HTML vocabulary, or any other available vocabularies.

With XSLT, you can create Processing Instructions using the *xsl : processing-instruction* element. However, you cannot use it to make XML declarations. With XPath, you can have a *processing-instruction ( )* node test. However, it cannot return and find the content of XML declarations.

Conclusion

Thank you again for purchasing this book!

I hope this book was able to help you use XML in your computing tasks.

The next step is to put the things you have learned into practice - try using XML to improve your web development project. Even if you're not really into creating websites, rest assured that there's a possible use of the markup language in your industry. Don't hesitate to share your knowledge with your friends and colleagues.

Finally, if you enjoyed this book, please take the time to share your thoughts and post a review on Amazon. We do our best to reach out to readers and provide the best value we can. Your positive review will help us achieve that. It'd be greatly appreciated!

Thank you and good luck!

Check Out My Other Books

Below you'll find some of my other popular books that are popular on Amazon and Kindle as well. Simply click on the links below to check them out. Alternatively, you can visit my author page on Amazon to see other work done by me.

Android Programming in a Day

Python Programming in a Day

C Programming Success in a Day

C Programming Professional Made Easy

JavaScript Programming Made Easy

PHP Programming Professional Made Easy

C ++ Programming Success in a Day

Windows 8 Tips for Beginners

HTML Professional Programming Made Easy

If the links do not work, for whatever reason, you can simply search for these titles on the Amazon website to find them.

Made in the USA
Lexington, KY
25 February 2016